Cast the First Stone

Be Transformed by Grace

5 Lessons to Discover the
Irrepressible Grace of Jesus

The Irrepressible Disciple Series
Book 2

Mary Rodman

Mary Rodman

Published by:
Legacy Lane Publishing
Weatherford, TX
www.LegacyLanePublishing.com
ISBN: 978-1-7352596-8-0

How to use this Bible study

I encourage you to spend time in prayer before and after each lesson. Ask God to open your mind and soul to the message before you start. Seek His blessings as you apply the lesson to your life afterward.

I encourage you to take notes as you read and contemplate the questions. I am a firm believer that it is a journaling is a wonderful concept, so grab a journal and record your thoughts! It leaves a path of your Christian journey, which you can read over and over.

Your Bible study can be used one of two ways.

1. **Individually** - Read one lesson each day or allow more time between the lessons to apply God's truths to your life.

2. **Group** - One or two lessons each week are recommended. Conversations and discussions with others will always provide more insight on the lessons. You will be amazed how each message speaks differently to others.

Please follow me on Social Media as **MrsMaryRodman** and leave a comment at www.facebook.com/MrsMaryRodman. I love to meet new people and will answer any questions you may have.

Enjoy your Bible study!

Mary

Mary Rodman

Table of Contents

Mary Rodman

Lesson 1: Defining Moments

Did you ever wish you could treat your life like text in a Word document? You simply highlight the moment and press the delete key. Poof! Gone—removed from your life forever. If it were only that simple, right? God disagrees with this concept because He chose you and I to experience the tragedy, or the hardship, or walk through the difficult situations in life for a reason. That is how He molds us into the people we are today.

There are also times in our lives when we think, "Wow God is so good to me. I didn't deserve His blessing today." I love those unexpected moments, both good and bad, which define us and help us grow in our relationship with Christ.

Often, we need to look at our past, to see into our future. Every moment from the past has brought you to where you are today. It doesn't matter if the bad defining moments outweigh the good ones in your life. You are here at this current moment in time for a reason.

Queen Esther is the perfect example of someone who suddenly found herself in the midst of a difficult defining moment. Mordecai requested that she appear before King Xerxes to save the lives of the Jewish people. If Esther requested to see the king when he had not called for her, it put her in a life-threatening position. So, Esther had a challenging decision to make, risk her own life, or risk the lives of the Jewish people. Not exactly the situation any of us would want to be in, but I love Mordecai's response to her.

Read *Esther 4:13-14*

After much prayer and preparation, Queen Esther appeared before King Xerxes, and the Jewish people were saved. How was she able to stand strong and confident in this situation? She understood that God would be with her when she approached King Xerxes. Plus, she knew that God loved her and was crazy about her.

Read *Isaiah 62:4*

In this passage of scripture, Isaiah is praying for the people of Jerusalem. Esther also knew these words to be true, and understood God had chosen her for a great assignment. These words are also a message to us today. A message of God's unending love for His people.

Regardless of your past or your current situation, *"The Lord delights in you." (Isaiah 62:4 NLT)*. God is absolutely crazy about you. He loves your smile, your abilities, your idiosyncrasies, and even your flaws, because when you wrap them all together—they make you. Wonderfully, uniquely made you. The person He created to accomplish great missions here on earth.

Read *Matthew 10:30-31*
Read *Psalm 56:8*

1. God knows every hair on your head. He catches every one of your tears! How do these verses change your vision of God's passion for you?

His love is so deep that all of your bad defining moments will one day be used for good. He has a great plan for your life, and that includes each experience you have had and will have, whether good or bad. Remember, no one else on earth is exactly like you and no one else on earth is here to do what God created you to do.

2. When you reflect on the bad moments in your life, do you understand why God allowed you to go through these experiences?

Some say that bad defining moments should be swept away, hidden, never to be talked about again. But God will change those bad moments in your life into good one day. If you disagree, please don't toss this study aside. Hang in there with me and you will understand where I'm coming from. I promise.

3. Do you agree or disagree that there are no bad defining moments in your life? Why?

Read *John 8:1-11*

The adulterous woman felt like an unworthy outcast. The Bible doesn't tell us of her sorted past, but there were most likely moments in her life which caused her to become a promiscuous woman. This particular time, she didn't hide her act of adultery in the dark of the night. She was caught and dragged out into the street in the middle of the day.

Many of us can relate to this woman. We have experienced the shame and humiliation she felt that day. Our sins may not be on public display, but they are very real within our own hearts, where we often hide our deepest pain.

4. Recall a bad defining moment in your life and how you felt about the situation. (You may or may not want to share this information in a group setting. That is okay, but please focus on the moment and see how God might transform it into good.)

Read *Romans 3:21-24*

5. How does this passage of scripture help you understand that God can turn the bad defining moments into good in your life?

As humans we categorize our sins, because of the consequences we face. In God's eyes, sin is sin. The good news is that God's grace is available for everyone, regardless of the sin. He doesn't pick and choose who to forgive or what to forgive. He forgives ALL confessed sins. So, this horrible defining moment in your life is no greater sin than the sin of forgetting to pray, or the sin of overindulgence.

6. Reflecting of the bad defining moment in your life which you looked at earlier, how can you apply this scripture and understand how and why God will one day turn that moment into good?

Before you answer, you may want to reread *Romans 3:23-24*.

Yes, the woman caught in adultery had a horrible defining moment in her life which she would rather forget. Being caught and dragged into the street is not a moment to remember with pride and joy. However, this horrible moment will ultimately lead her to the hand of grace. As we continue with this study, we will look more into grace, because grace is the heart of God. But first we need to understand her shame and humiliation in the next lesson.

Your Challenge

As I stated earlier, there are both good and bad defining moments in your life. Focus on both before the next lesson. What defining moments, both good and bad, in your life have shaped you into the person you are today? Because, *"Who knows if perhaps you were made queen for just such a time as this?" (Esther 4:14).*

Journal your thoughts on this lesson.

Circle of Faith

Faith is an element in my life, which I have questioned from time to time. What exactly is faith? *Hebrews 11:1 (NIV)* says "*Faith is confidence in what we hope for and assurance about what we do not see.*" If I pray for something in faith and it doesn't happen, is that a lack of faith? I have come to realize over the years that it is not. We need to understand and be thankful that God sometimes says, "No."

I grew up in a godly home where examples of faith surrounded me. On the family farm, there was a great deal of work, but there were also lessons of faith. I watched year after year as my father planted the seed and had faith it would grow. The seed needed to receive the right amount of rain, sunshine, and nutrients to produce a crop, which provided food for his dairy cattle and an income for his family.

I observed my mother, who was definitely a *Proverbs 31* woman. She had the faith necessary to stretch Dad's income to provide for their five children. Her faith showed her how to be a farm wife, gardener, seamstress, nurse, cook, and mother. As a young wife and mother, she had faith in herself and God through many of life's challenges. Faith God would give her strength for each new day and help her provide for the needs of her family.

As a very little girl, I remember my Grandpa Robinson quoting scripture to his grandchildren. I didn't realize it, but he was teaching us the importance of knowing God's Word.

I have fond memories of my Grandma Conklin, who invested in my life. She not only spoiled me like any grandma does, she showed me what it was like to be active in her church. She invested herself in the lives of others by teaching Sunday school, preparing dinners at the church, and many other activities with the ladies. No matter how tired she was, she always saved the end of the day for prayer and reading her Bible. As a young child, I observed her, and remembered all of this information. She molded me, and left a huge imprint on my heart by her examples.

We attended Sunday school and church every Sunday. I knew the Bible stories like all the other children at church. It just didn't take root in my heart as a tangible part of my life. In spite of all this wonderful upbringing, I had to find faith in God on my own. It wasn't until I came to the end of myself, that I found a lifeline to sustain me. Christ became my hope and my future.

After my divorce and struggling as a single mother of two, I found myself looking back to my roots. My bad choices in life had piled on top of one another, until the only place left to look was up. I sat on my sofa one lonely evening and cried out to God. I found myself wrapped in His loving arms as I asked Him to give my life new purpose and direction. It was a private time between God and myself, as I rededicated my life to Him that tearful night. The following morning, I had a new confidence in myself and my life, because it was now in Christ's hands. I knew from the faith examples of my family that God would not let me down. The path ahead may be rocky, but it would be the right one, because God was leading for the first time in my adult life.

Unknown to me, following his divorce, my husband, Jim, was praying for a companion in his life. God heard our prayers and set us on a path to meet one another. The rest is history, as we have now been married for twenty-eight years. He is the love of my life, and he took me back to my roots— the farm. Of course, there have been rough days, squabbles, and hard work on the farm. In spite of any problems we encounter, we never lose focus of the fact that God brought two lonely, messed up lives together. God took what we called a mess, and made it something beautiful.

I was blessed with more Christian roots as well. I was given a mother-in-law who taught me more lessons in faith. No matter the circumstances, problem, or decision we faced on the farm Leah would say, "We just need to have faith and pray."

Her faith in God shined as she walked daily with the Lord, and was a faithful prayer warrior. She went home to be with the Lord many years ago and Jim often says he misses the daily prayers he knows his mother said on his behalf.

My faith has taken me full circle in life. Our sons were raised on the farm, are both in the agriculture business, and are also involved the family farm. Jim and I have tried to instill in their lives the importance of faith in God from the smallest decision, to the biggest one. I thank God that He took my messed-up life, and set my feet on the right path. As a result, my children were surrounded with the same godly foundation and roots by which I was raised.

As life goes full circle, I look forward to being a mentor of faith to my daughters-in-law. I pray that one day my grandchildren will see me saving the end of every day for Jesus, or hear me quote a Bible verse. I want to plant seeds of faith in their hearts as they grow. I pray that I have successfully planted seeds of faith in my sons which will sustain them. One lonely evening, they too may journey to the sofa, and Christ will become a more tangible part of their lives. My hope is that the circle of faith will continue for many generations and we continue to share Leah's familiar words, "We just need to have faith and pray."

Excerpt from *Bloom Where You're Planted*

Mary's greatest joy is helping others cultivate and grow their relationship with Christ. Part of her ministry is her devotional books: *Bloom Where You're Planted* and *Live Life in Full Bloom*. Purchase your *Bloom Daily Devotional Series* books with matching journals at www.MaryRodman.com/Shop.

Lesson 2: The Shame

A little review on where we left off in our story from Lesson 1. According to the law of Moses, adultery was a crime which was punishable by death. Both parties should have been stoned, yet the Pharisees only ridiculed this woman. She didn't hide her act of sin in the dark of the night. The Pharisees caught her in the act of adultery during the day and dragged her out into the street as a sinner who deserved death.

They found great pleasure in humiliating her in front of Jesus and the rest of the onlookers. Not only had she been caught in the act of adultery, the Pharisees used her like a pawn in a game. Their objective had nothing to do with her sins. Their scheme was to trick Jesus on the meaning of the law.

Reread *John 8:3*

Shame. Humiliation. Disgrace. Brokenhearted. Sin. Pain. Hatred. Insulted. Mocked.

1. Can you relate to the agony of the adulterous woman? Recall the bad defining moment which you looked at in Lesson 1. List the emotions you felt or still feel as a result of your blunder.

You talk about defining moments! All the sins in her life were suddenly exposed to a large crowd, in a public place, and before this man everyone talked about, named Jesus. I see her lying on the ground, curled up in a ball, with tears streaming down her face. Possibly her arms around her head as she protected herself from the stones, which would soon strike her body. Every emotion within her was now bubbling out as she was put on public display and humiliated in front of a group of onlookers.

Read *Psalm 69:1*

2. Do you think this woman knew Jesus was the son of God? Would she have possibly said words similar to Psalm 69:1? Explain your answer.

Unfortunately, we have no way knowing if she knew who Jesus was before this encounter. Regardless, I'm sure she was longing for protection from the Pharisees. Not only was she dealing with humiliation and fear, her life was in danger!

We can relate to the emotions she was experiencing, because we too are broken people. We are going to look at a couple of *Psalms* in this lesson, because they provide wisdom and comfort when our emotions are running wild. There is comfort in these verses, whether you are being judged by others, or you are judging yourself, as we often do.

As you read the scripture verses, remember this woman was being used like a pawn in a game. The Pharisees didn't care about her sin. If they were truly concerned about her act of adultery, they would have also dragged the man into the street to be stoned. She most likely had a reputation in the town for the lascivious life style she lived. But now public humiliation was added to her list of troubles, simply so the Pharisees could attempt to trap Jesus.

Humiliation and Insults: Read *Psalm 69:7*

Sin: Read *Psalm 69:12-13*

Hatred: Read *Psalm 69:14*

Shame: Read *Psalm 69:19-20*

Pain and Suffering: Read *Psalm 69:29*

3. As she laid at Jesus' feet, do you think she prayed for God to rescue her from her sins, the hatred, the shame and the pain she was experiencing?

Psalm 69 is one of the most quoted *Psalms* in the Old Testament. It is often applied to the suffering of Jesus himself. He too understood the same rejection, pain, and suffering which the adulterous woman experienced. In this situation alone, the Pharisees were mocking Him and demanding an answer. We will look more into Jesus' reaction to their demands in Lesson 4. For now, please understand His great compassion for this woman who was tossed at His feet like a useless human being.

Mocked and Disgraced: Read *Psalm 89:49-51*

There she was in the public square being mocked and disgraced. Shame surrounded her like a cloud which would never lift. Was she looking for love in the wrong place? Did she know enough about God to question His sovereignty? You talk about your bad defining moments in life—this one tops them all!

Our sin doesn't have to be an act of adultery to understand these same emotions. When we make mistakes, we often feel as if the entire world has turned on us. It is important that we remember where to turn when we are brokenhearted. There is peace when we turn to Jesus with a repentant heart.

Brokenhearted: Read *Psalm 34:17-19*

4. When you come to the end of yourself, where do you look for help? Where should you look for help?

The adulterous woman experienced every emotion known as she cowered at the feet of Jesus. As you have already read in the complete story, she is about to receive the hand of grace, but at this point and time, she doesn't know what her future holds. Are the stones about to hit her body, or will this man they call Jesus protect her?

I call this a "Maryism" because I don't have scripture to support my thoughts. I believe she prayed and asked God to spare her life. If Jesus is about to extend her the hand of grace, He had to know her heart. At that moment, she may not have understood Jesus was the son of God, but she only had one place left to turn with her broken life—God.

Oh, the emotions, the agony, and the shame we often carry when we don't take our troubles to the Lord. We sometimes allow ourselves to hit rock bottom before we reach out to Him. Don't go through life with a broken spirit. Remember, *"The Lord delights in you." (Isaiah 62:4).*

Apply these wonderful words written by the psalmist David to your own life. Carry them in your heart as a reminder that God is here to rescue you from the bad defining moments in your life. Why? Because *"The Lord is close to the brokenhearted; he rescues those whose spirits are crushed. (Psalm 34:18)*

Your Challenge

For God to turn your bad defining moments into good, you too have to come to the feet of Jesus and seek His compassion and forgiveness. Write a prayer in your journal asking God to reveal any hidden emotions from your past or current situations and heal your broken heart.

Journal your thoughts on this lesson.

Peeling the Layers

When I was a kid, I loved helping Mom peel the wallpaper from the walls. It was fun in the old house to see how many layers you could find, or even what the layer below looked like. Many times, the wall underneath was cracked and we were surprised at all the problems we found. On occasion, Mom had to call in a professional to repair the walls. But other times, the layer below was prettier than the one on top and we wondered why someone covered such beauty. The best part of the project was always the end result, a room which was clean and renewed with beauty.

Wallpaper layers remind me of the layers of our lives. Good and bad childhood memories, followed by the painful teenage years. Marriage or maybe the lack of a marriage. Possibly even the loss of a loved one or parent. Life can also be topped with hurtful words from a friend, possibly the loss of a job or a divorce. We face so many trials in a lifetime, but how we face those challenges can be the difference between the layers we hide behind, and the layers we peel off.

To me, God is my Professional. No matter what the trial is in my life, He shows up just when I need Him. He fills the cracks in my broken life! When I struggled after my divorce, He set my feet back on His path. He gave me strength to be a single parent and to start each day knowing His forgiveness and grace.

More importantly, God peels off my layers of shame, hurt, shyness and bitterness. I love to carry around all my layers. They feel like a safe haven I can hide behind. But the truth is, they are ugly! Once I let God peel off these layers, I find myself, the person God designed me to be. Christ often peels off our layers to find beautiful hidden talents, which we have buried behind years of cover up and lack of confidence.

In *John 8:1–11*, we read how the Pharisees brought a woman who was caught in adultery before Jesus. They wanted to stone her, as was the custom in the Law of Moses. Jesus started to peel the layers off of the Pharisees and her! He asked who among them was without sin. The Pharisees realized that none of them could cast the first stone, as they were all guilty of sin. I like to think that the Pharisees had a moment of guilty conscious, as they slowly walked away.

But let's focus on the layers of guilt and shame from the woman. She had lived a very sinful life, but she understood that God had forgiven her. God didn't tell her to go hide behind the layers of her past. Instead He said, *"Go and sin no more." (John 8:11).* He peeled off those layers of guilt with forgiveness as she acknowledged Jesus as Lord.

My prayer for you today is that you allow Christ to peel off the layers of your life. It will feel so good to see the beauty underneath as you make Him the Lord of your life.

Excerpt from *Bloom Where You're Planted*

Read more of my favorite devotions from *Bloom Where You're Planted* at www.maryrodman.com/BookBonuses. These free devotions from the *Bloom Daily Devotional Series* will enlighten and brighten your relationship with Christ.

Lesson 3: The Judgement

We left the woman caught in adultery at Jesus' feet, cowering in fear with every emotion raging. Remember, she is simply a pawn in the game the Pharisees are playing with Jesus. They don't really care about her sins. In Lesson 2, we focused on the woman and her many emotions. Now our focus turns to the Pharisees. You may want to reread the entire section of scripture before you begin.

Reread *John 8:1-11*

1. Has there been a time in your life when you judged someone for their questionable actions? Especially in a group setting—sometimes in the "name of love," otherwise known as gossip.

There was a love-hate relationship between the Pharisees and Jesus. The Pharisees did not believe Jesus was the Messiah and felt it was their "duty" to continually attack His ways. Jesus on the other hand is love, so even though the Pharisees were constantly against Him, He still loved them. The Pharisees taught by rules and regulations. Jesus taught with compassion, healing, and love. He didn't care about all their manmade rules, and He was not about to give into their demands. Jesus wanted the Pharisees to change their narrow-minded thinking and have repentant hearts.

The Pharisees designed a scheme to trap Jesus. The Jewish people were not permitted to carry out their own executions. So, if Jesus told them to stone the woman, they could report him to the Romans. If Jesus told them not to kill her, He was breaking the law of Moses. *(Deuteronomy 22:22)*. Their only objective was to prove Jesus wrong. What they didn't expect was for Jesus to turn the situation against them, forcing them to answer their own question.

> *"Teacher," they said to Jesus, "this woman was caught in the act of adultery. The law of Moses says to stone her. What do you say?" (John 8:4-5)*

Read *James 5:9*

2. Why should we and the Pharisees not judge one another according to this scripture?

The Pharisees had a huge case of ego as they looked past their own sins and judged the adulterous woman. Even though they were trained in the scriptures, they preferred to ignore the fact that they too had sins in their lives. Often, we fall into the same trap. It is much easier for us to look at the inadequacies of someone else, than to look at our own sinful ways.

Reread *John 8:9*

I find it interesting that the scriptures say the oldest and wisest of them left first. Yes, I believe we become wiser with age, but wisdom also comes from reading and understanding the scriptures.

Read *James 1:5*

Read *Proverbs 2:6*

3. As you mature in your Christian walk, do you feel you have become less judgmental of others? Is that due to godly wisdom?

4. Why did the Pharisees suddenly have a change of heart about stoning the woman?

Even though they desperately wanted to trap Jesus, one by one, they quickly realized that they too were guilty of sin. They were not perfect, therefore none of them could *Cast the First Stone*.

Read *James 2:12-13*

Once again, Jesus teaches the Pharisees the meaning of grace. The law is a set of rules, which we can never completely obey. Grace frees us from the law, but because the Holy Spirit lives within us, our desire is to obey the law. The Pharisees were forced to take a good look at their own sins and walk away.

5. How does *James 2:13* compare the way the Pharisees treated the adulterous woman, versus how we should treat others who have sinned?

Mercy—we are called to show one another mercy, just as God shows us mercy. Until we learn the power of forgiveness and show others empathy for their sins, we will be unable to forgive ourselves.

Your Challenge

Memorize the life changing verse below. We need to extend the hand of grace and show mercy to others, just like Christ offers us grace. Often, forgiveness begins by forgiving ourselves for the bad defining moments in our lives. How will this scripture impact your outlook on the sins of others and yourself in the future?

No, O people, the Lord has told you what is good, and this is what he requires of you: to do what is right, to love mercy, and to walk humbly with your God. (Micah 6:8)

Journal your thoughts on this lesson.

God's Love

Did you ever notice that the longer you know someone the more alike you become? On most days, I can finish my husband's sentences or even know what funny comment he is about to make. I find the longer we are married the more alike we become and the more I love him.

No matter how well we know and love our spouses, our children, or our best friend, it is nothing compared to how well God knows us and loves us! The Bible tells us, *"The very hairs on your head are all numbered. So don't be afraid; you are more valuable to God than a whole flock of sparrows." (Luke 12:7).* Just imagine how well He knows you to have numbered the hairs on your head!

Jeremiah 1:5a (MSG) goes on to say, *"Before I shaped you in the womb, I knew all about you. Before you saw the light of day, I had holy plans for you."* I have made many mistakes in my life yet God approves of me with all of my flaws!

Just as my husband woos me, God woos us. He longs to have a relationship with us. No sin we have committed is too great to keep us from His love.

When children misbehave, they instinctively run and hide from their parents. No matter whether you hide temporarily or a long time, you hide because you feel unworthy of love. In either situation, a child knows there is unconditional love in the arms of their parent and they eventually return.

This is much like our relationship with Christ. We are God's children who ask for forgiveness from their Father. Sometimes it's easy to ask for mercy and other times we question why Christ would forgive us for all we have done. Nothing you and I do will ever keep us from the love of God. He will always forgive all our sins, if we simply return to His arms of grace. *"There is forgiveness of sins for all who repent." (Luke 24:47b)*.

This is my prayer for you today, *"May the Lord direct your heart into God's love and Christ's perseverance." (2 Thessalonians 3:5 NIV)*. If you don't know Christ or if you walked away from him, please take time to pray and ask him for the forgiveness of your sins. Abba Father longs to hold you close and have a relationship with you.

Excerpt from *Live Life in Full Bloom*

As a speaker, Mary is known for her humor, and inspirational messages which challenge you to walk daily with Jesus. Book Mary for your next event at www.MaryRodman.com/speaking.

Lesson 4: Patience of Christ

In the first lesson, I challenged you to look at the defining moments in your life. In lesson 2, we studied the emotions, the fear, and the humiliation on the adulterous woman. Then in lesson 3, we flipped it around and did a self-examination of our own actions toward others, because we often act much like the Pharisees.

Now we will focus on the patience of Christ. WWJD—What would Jesus do? Even though this is an old saying, it is appropriate in this situation. How did He reply to the demands of the Pharisees?

"The law of Moses says to stone her. What do you say?" (John 8:5).

The Pharisees were angry at Jesus, so this was a stern question, not one where they were simply searching for an opinion. Jesus had no reason to quickly give in to their demands, and refused to answer them immediately. Time was on His side as He patiently waited before speaking.

1. Have you ever patiently waited for God to answer a prayer, or maybe you still are? How does waiting on God impact your life?

Read *John 8:6*

Put yourself in the position of the Pharisees for a few moments. Even though they relied heavily on their own manmade rules, they were very knowledgeable in the scriptures. They were sure Jesus would give an immediate answer based on the Word of God. But, Jesus ignored their demands, instead He stooped down and wrote in the sand. In His own quiet way, Jesus taught them the importance of waiting patiently on the Lord.

Read *Psalm 27:14*

2. How does this verse change your outlook as you patiently (or maybe impatiently) wait for the Lord to answer your prayers?

Read *Lamentations 3:25-26*

Waiting on the Lord is often very difficult. Sometimes we act like the Pharisees and demand immediate answers. But these verses tell us that it is good to wait for the Lord and to search for answers.

Just like the Pharisees, God often says, "Be patient my child." He uses these periods of waiting to teach us and strengthen us. Waiting makes us courageous and builds our faith and trust.

There are different opinions on what Jesus wrote in the sand that day. Some say He wrote scripture to convict the Pharisees. Others say He wrote the names of her accusers.

My favorite speculation is that He actually wrote the word forgiveness, because He was about to teach the true meaning of grace. Regardless of what he wrote, the Pharisees definitely were not expecting the answer they received.

Read *John 8:7-8*

I love how The Message reads for this passage. *"The sinless one among you, go first: Throw the stone." (John 8:7 MSG)*. This passage sounds as if Jesus is taunting the Pharisees, daring them to even pick up a stone. His reply was probably just as stern as their question, as He protected the woman.

This part amazes me. What does Jesus do next? He writes in the sand again! Maybe this time, Jesus actually wrote the names of those who were overlooking their own sins. Possibly He wanted to give the Pharisees more time to contemplate their actions.

What a defining moment for the Pharisees. Jesus' patience forced them to examine their own lives. They instantly went from demanding and forceful to timid and meek.

The Pharisees knowledge of the scriptures, combined with Jesus patiently writing in the sand forced them to evaluate their own lives. When Jesus forced them to look at their hypocritical ways, He left them with no other choice but to leave. They couldn't stone her, because they too had sinned.

Read *Psalm 40:1-3*

3. Reflecting on your answer to the first question in this lesson. Do these verses give you more hope as you patiently wait for answers to your prayers?

Times of waiting on God can seem almost unbearable. Yet those are the moments when He teaches us the most. The Pharisees were impatient, demanding, judgmental, and strict about the rules and regulations. By quietly waiting before Jesus answered their question, He forced them to calm down and reflect on their own inadequacies. What a moment of conviction when they realized how imperfect they truly were!

Likewise, God desires for you to wait patiently on Him. During moments of waiting, the Lord will refresh your faith, strengthen your hope, and renew your spirit. While you wait, remember His timing is perfect and His answers are divine.

Wait patiently for the Lord.
Be brave and courageous.
Yes, wait patiently for the Lord.
Psalm 27:14

Your Challenge

Summarize how the first four lessons impacted your life. How can your bad defining moments be turned to good? Do you relate to the emotions of the adulterous woman? Do you judge others like the Pharisees did? Can you turn any of these situations or emotions around for good when waiting patiently for the Lord?

Journal your thoughts on this lesson.

The Cabin

While on vacation, we rented a cabin for a couple of nights. The location was great, tucked back against the mountain and secluded. There was a wraparound porch which I enjoyed each evening as I sat and read a book. When we returned from our travels one afternoon, we were even greeted by three deer in the horse corral behind the cabin. They were apparently accustomed to vehicles and people because our arrival didn't bother them in the least. The inside of the cabin was well equipped with cooking utensils, laundry facilities, and all the usual amenities of home.

What bothered us about the cabin were the decorations. It seemed to be over decorated. The décor was fitting, but there was no place for our "stuff." If there was a corner or a table, there was a knickknack tucked away, and in most cases two or three. We even chuckled when we found a moose statue on the bed post of our log headboard. I know decorating is a personal preference. What appeared as clutter to us would be beauty to someone else.

It is the same with God. What appears to be clutter in our lives, God sees as beauty. The sins of our past, our bad choices, ungodly decisions throughout our lives can clutter our minds and clutter our hearts making us feel unworthy.

The Israelites had a lot of clutter in their lives. They were the product of slavery. God freed them, but they still had a slavery mentality. As I mentioned in the previous devotional, they did a lot of whining and complaining. Far worse than their whining and complaining was their lack of commitment to follow God wholeheartedly.

While Moses was on Mount Sinai receiving the Ten Commandments, they persuaded Aaron to build them a Golden Calf to worship. *(Exodus 32:1-6)*. They rebelled against Joshua and Caleb when they wanted to go conquer the Promised Land. *(Joshua 14:1-12)*. They would continuously repent, and then disobey God again. Rather than driving the people out of the Promised Land, they made treaties with them and allowed their altars to foreign gods stay in the land. As a result, the next generation of Israelites were soon worshiping Baal. *(Judges 2:1-4, 10-15)*. The list could go on and on about the clutter in the hearts and the lives of the Israelites.

No matter the sins of the Israelites, their bad decisions, or their ungodly choices, God never gave up on them. Yes—God allowed them to be taken into exile, but more importantly, God rescued them.

This is what the Lord says: "You will be in Babylon for seventy years. But then I will come and do for you all the good things I have promised, and I will bring you home again. For I know the plans I have for you," says the Lord. "They are plans for good and not for disaster, to give you a future and a hope. In those days when you pray, I will listen. If you look for me wholeheartedly, you will find me. I will be found by you," says the Lord. "I will end your captivity and restore your fortunes. I will gather you out of the nations where I sent you and will bring you home again to your own land." (Jeremiah 29:10-14)

Like the Israelites, God longs to end your captivity of the clutter in your life. He is patiently waiting for you to seek Him wholeheartedly. God's promises are timeless. Remember God's words, *"I have promised, and I will bring you home again."* Come to Him today and leave the clutter of your life behind knowing God has plans *"to give you a future and a hope."*

Excerpt from *Bloom in God's Promises*

Bloom in God's Promises is the third book in the *Bloom Daily Devotional Series*. Follow Mary on social media as MrsMaryRodman. Please like my Facebook page: https://facebook.com/MrsMaryRodman.

Lesson 5: Irrepressible Grace

In previous lessons, we looked at the horrible defining moment of the adulterous woman. That moment she was put on public display, humiliated and shamed at the feet of Jesus. The Pharisees—their demanding attitude toward Jesus, combined with their many rules and regulations, which made them so hypocritical. Yet Jesus with all of His patience, stooped down to write in the sand. He forced the Pharisees to do a self-examination of their own lives, and walk away.

Now comes my favorite part of the entire story. *The Irrepressible Grace of Jesus!* In order to get the full impact of the last lesson, please reread the entire story.

Reread *John 8:1-11*

I love *John 8:9b. "Only Jesus was left in the middle of the crowd with the woman."* This is her face to face moment with Jesus. Where the rubber meets the road. Her life changing event is about to take place. How will she react? What will she say?

Reread *John 8:10*

1. How to you think the woman reacted when Jesus spoke to her?

Remember her promiscuous life style? Her self-worth was on the bottom of the scale. No one ever treated her with kindness, yet Jesus spoke to her. She had to be shocked!

I see the boundaries of shame and embarrassment slowly come down. She probably uncurled her body enough to lift her head and gaze up at Him in awe. Looking around, she noticed all of her accusers had vanished. Then she realized that Jesus was actually speaking to her.

She had just been accused of adultery, which was punishable by death. Plus, she had experienced the worst defining moment of her life! Why would He possibly protect her and risk being ridiculed for associating with her? None of that matters to Jesus as He said, *"Where are your accusers?" (John 8:10).*

Reflect back to Lesson 1 and the bad defining moment in your life. Now put yourself in the position of this woman, and Jesus is speaking to you.

2.   Who and where are your accusers?

I envision Jesus reaching to help the woman to her feet. Slowly she looks around in astonishment and exclaims, "They are gone!"

In an instant, her life was spared. No more accusers. No more embarrassment. No more fear. No more shame. No more disgrace. But now what? How long until someone else tries to humiliate her?

When Jesus reached **down** to help her, He reached **out** with the hand of irrepressible grace!

Reread *John 8:10-11*

3. Notice my emphasis on the words **down** and **out**. How are they different?

Christ never ***reaches down*** to us or ***looks down*** at us. He reaches ***out*** to save us. No matter where you and I are, or what we have done, He reaches ***out*** to rescue us. We could feel like we are in a sinking pit, or possibly we are falling from a mountain top experience. Our lives could be like hurricane winds, swirling at high speeds. It doesn't matter how we got there. Christ never looks ***down*** upon our lives, but He will always reach ***out*** to save us.

Read *Romans 6:23*

The woman caught in adultery was a sinner who lived a promiscuous lifestyle, and according to the law of Moses she should have been killed. That didn't matter to Jesus. Instead, He reached ***out*** and offered her the gift of grace.

Read *Ephesians 2:8-9*

4. Why would Jesus offer her grace in this situation?

Read *1 John 5:1*

5. Why do you deserve the same grace as the adulterous woman?

Jesus extended her the hand of grace that day, but He also commanded her to leave her life of sin. The Bible doesn't tell us what her decision was, but I believe she chose grace. Jesus saved her life, an act of kindness she undoubtedly would never forget.

She didn't deserve grace and neither do we. It is a free gift from God, for all who believe that Jesus is their Savior. We can't earn grace with our good works. We can't purchase grace for a price, because Jesus already paid the price when He died at Calvary. The only thing we can do is trade our nasty ugly sins for His amazing grace.

Read *Romans 10:9, 10, 13*

In a short period of time, this woman had two defining moments in her life.

The bad—The moment the Pharisees humiliated her and dragged her out into public using her like a pawn in a game to trap Jesus.

The good—The moment Jesus reached ***out*** and offered her irrepressible grace.

We don't know what the woman chose, but life is about choices. When you feel like you are a failure in life, I pray that you too will accept Christ's hand of grace. The greatest decision you will ever make is to follow Jesus, and continually seek His forgiveness.

Read *2 Corinthians 5:17*

Remember our Word document from Lesson 1—that horrible moment in your life which you wanted to highlight and delete? Well good news, when you confess your sins to Jesus, he wipes the slate clean. Poof! That horrible defining moment is truly gone and a new life has begun!

Jesus will transform your life of sin into something beautiful. For the person doing this study who claimed a bad defining moment could never be turned into good, I hope you now understand how God can wipe the slate clean, and change your life into a beautiful tapestry.

We all have experiences we would like to delete, but without those moments of despair, how would we know our hope is in Jesus!

Read *Romans 15:13*

6. How can you use this confident hope to be a witness to God's irrepressible grace?

Irrepressible Grace—There is no better way to turn your bad defining moments into good. One day God will use each and every part of your life as you become a witness of His grace. Remember, there is only one you, which has experienced these moments. There is only one you, with your unique personality. Greatest of all, there is only one you, who was created to do exactly what God has called you to do.

As you apply these 5 lessons to your life, remember these important truths.

- *"Who knows if perhaps you were made queen for just such a time as this?" (Esther 4:14).* God created you for a reason and a purpose. Remember, *"The Lord delights in you." (Isaiah 62:4).* (Lesson 1).
- *"The Lord is close to the brokenhearted." (Psalm 34:18).* Jesus hears your cry of pain when you feel buried under a life of sin. He is there for you, night and day. (Lesson 2).
- *"This is what he requires of you: to do what is right, to love mercy, and to walk humbly with your God." (Micah 6:8).* Don't be quick to judge. Show others and especially yourself mercy. (Lesson 3).
- *"Yes, wait patiently for the Lord." (Psalm 27:14).* Life changes when we wait patiently for the Lord, because that is how He teaches us to depend on Him. (Lesson 4).
- *"Thank you for making me so wonderfully complex! Your workmanship is marvelous—how well I know it." (Psalm 139:14).* There is only one unique you, who God created for a purpose. Don't waste the defining moments in your life, use both the good and the bad experiences for God's glory. (Lesson 5).

God created you. Wonderfully, uniquely made you, to experience all the tragedies, trials, and wonders in your life. All for a reason and with a purpose in mind.

Like the adulterous woman, the decision is now yours. Will you choose to follow Jesus and sin no more, or will you choose to walk away from the One who can lift you out of a life of despair? I pray you choose to walk the road of hope together with Jesus!

Your Challenge

What is your decision? Will you accept the hand of grace and live your life with Jesus daily? How can you share *The Irrepressible Grace of Jesus* with others?

Journal your thoughts on this lesson.

A Free Woman

Christ set Mary Magdalene free from seven demons! As a result of this freedom, she continually shows her appreciation for God's sovereignty. This dramatic change in her life continually brought her back to the feet of Jesus. Her newly found freedom, combined with her servant's heart and financial abilities made her a thankful, behind the scenes worker for Jesus!

Many of us take the freedom from our sins for granted. God's grace offers us this freedom so we no longer have to carry the burden of our sinful life. After Christ set Mary Magdalene free from seven demons, she never looked back. She continually looked forward as a servant of Christ.

Jesus Christ offers us this wonderful gift of grace. No one else can ever do this, because there is only one God and one Savior.

Mary Magdalene put her faith in Christ when He healed her from seven demons. Christ offers this free gift of salvation to all who call on His name.

Excerpt from
Mary Magdalene a Woman of Resilience
5 Lessons to Develop an Irrepressible Passion for Jesus

Mary Magdalene a Woman of Resilience is the first book in *The Irrepressible Servant Series*. How was Mary Magdalene able to overcome her demons to become the first witness of Christ's resurrection? Purchase your copy of this study today at www.MaryRodman.com/shop.

Resources

Discount Purchases

- My gift to you—Enter coupon code **ThankYou** at www.MaryRodman.com/shop to receive a **one-time only 20% discount** on any purchases from my website. All devotionals will be signed before shipment.

- *Bloom Daily Devotional Series Book 1, Bloom Where You're Planted*

  "This beautifully written book is a delight, filled with wonderful stories from her life and awesome applications of God's truth. It will lift you up and speak words of truth and encouragement into your life." *~Doris Swift*

- *Bloom Daily Devotional Series Book 2, Live Life in Full Bloom*

  "A must-read devotional. Mary's words are from her heart. I can see every story, as if I was standing there watching it happen. I laughed so hard at some of the stories because, life happens. ~TGJ – Amazon Customer

- *Bloom Where You're Planted Journal* Includes a quote from each devotion and a place to journal your thoughts, including a Daily Gratitude section.

- *Live Life in Full Bloom Journal* Daily Gratitude section and a highlight from each devotion.

- *The Irrepressible Disciple Series Book 1, Mary Magdalene a Woman of Resilience.*

  Mary Magdalene was transformed from a woman possessed by seven demons into a servant of Christ. Where did she find the resilience to sit at the foot of the cross on crucifixion day? 5 lessons to develop an irrepressible passion for Jesus.

Download free Resources for your next event

- Free devotions from *Bloom in God's Promises* at www.MaryRodman.com/SneakPeek

  Bloom in God's Promises Sneak Peek We often develop a negative attitude rather than counting our blessings. These devotions will help you look at the good side of life.

- Download free devotions from *Live Life in Full Bloom* at www.MaryRodman.com/BookBonus

  Live Life in Full Bloom Favorites. Devotions to help you see gratitude in your life and focus on God's will each day.

- Download the first devotional ever written by Mary at www.MaryRodman.com/BookBonuses

  "Fall Harvest" Our words and our attitude can impact those around us. You will find comfort in Leah's words of wisdom, "We just need to pray for patience and strength this time of year."

Book Mary as a Speaker-Facilitator for your weekend retreat at www.MaryRodman.com/speaking

- **Who Are You? Discover the Woman God Created You to Be** *"There are many virtuous and capable women in the world, but you surpass them all!" (Proverbs 31:29)*
- Mary's retreat will transform your walk with Christ as she shares her funny stories, biblical examples, and powerful messages through these four topics.

Defining Moments Within minutes, the Woman caught in adultery had both good and bad defining moments in her life. The moment she was dragged into public and humiliated, and the moment Jesus said, "Go and sin no more." Mary will challenge you to see both bad and good defining moments as good, when used for God's glory.

God Loves You The Samaritan Woman made many mistakes in her life, yet Jesus pursued her until she understood she was loved by the Savior of the world. Mary's words of encouragement will challenge you to serve Christ regardless of your past mistakes.

Who Are You? Mary Magdalene was possessed by seven evil spirits. Christ changed her life dramatically and she understood who she was in Christ and how to serve her Savior.

Dare to Dream Caleb dreamed of the Promised Land for over forty years, but patiently waited for the Lord to lead the battle to conquer the land. Your dreams will also come into fruition, when you align your dreams with God's will for your life.

- This weekend retreat is available in multiple formats.
  - Mary as a speaker. She will present the four talks and provide breakout questions for your small group leaders in advance.
  - Mary as both the speaker and the facilitator for your event.
  - Optional music by Angie Howard. Angie's musical talent as a worship leader and soloist is uplifting and inspirational.

Book Mary as a keynote speaker for your next event. Her topics include...

- **Something Out of Nothing** The loss of four family members in five years sent Mary into a season of grief. Grief is a true pain which sometimes feels unbearable. She shares how she made something out of nothing to move on with her life.
- ***Dare to Dream*** *Your dreams are simply dreams, unless we align them with God's will for your life. Mary will challenge you to accomplish great ministry when the Lord is with you. "What you dare to dream of, dare to do." Sarah Jane Shoaf.*
- ***Bloom Where You're Planted*** *From a wild ride down the mountainside to the heartaches of life, Mary shares how to BLOOM in all aspects of your life.*
- ***The Woman God Sees*** *God sees you as His chosen, precious, beloved, royalty. Learn how "The Lord delights in you. (Isaiah 62:4)." through Mary's personal stories intertwined with scripture.*
- ***A Christian Farm Wife's Perspective*** *As a newlywed on the farm Mary soon realized her life was much different than it was growing up on a dairy farm. She shares some of her stressful moments and how a Christ centered marriage makes a difference as they worked together.*
- ***Faith, Farming or Career?*** *Do you ever wonder which direction to turn? Why not include them all? Mary's strong faith is the pivotal point which merges her farm life with her career as a Christian writer and speaker. She shares farm statistics to increase awareness of the family farm along with her stories of strong faith as encouragement.*

Custom Topic Mary enjoys Bible research and sharing some of the antics from her life. She is open to speaking opportunities on your topic of choice. Please allow six-weeks preparation time, unless prior arrangements have been made. For more information go to www.MaryRodman.com/speaking.

More Books and Resources
by Mary Rodman

Stay in touch by using our messenger's treasury of transformational inspiration, insight, and guidance. **Download and join** the free *Inspire U app* for additional personal resources on your mobile device today!

Enjoy videos I recorded and placed in The Inspire U app associated with this book. They will bring you more insight into the 5 lessons and Irrepressible Grace.

Did you enjoy *Cast the First Stone?*
Then you should read
Mary Magdalene a Woman of Resilience

Mary Magdalene was transformed from a woman possessed by seven demons, into a resilient servant who sat at the foot of the cross on crucifixion day. She will inspire you to: Give from the heart. Serve graciously. Embrace your freedom. Live with gratitude. And witness for Jesus.

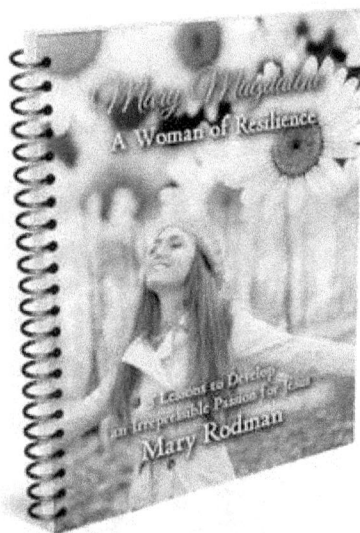

Bloom Daily Devotional Series.
Bloom Where You're Planted

Through laughter, memories and even sorrow, Mary helps you see the Bright Morning Star, named Jesus. Discover her humor in the devotional Bird Poop, as she highlights the Biblical example of Abigail and how you might handle unwelcome life circumstances.

Live Life in Full Bloom.

Chuckle as Mary shares her rotisserie experience at the sleep clinic, ad how she was humbly reminded of the blessings in her life which she had taken for granted.

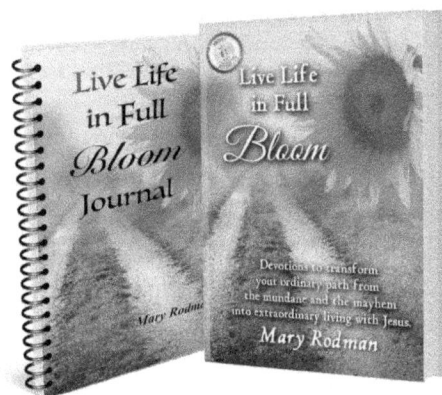

Bloom In God's Promises!

Read Mary's award winning devotional, "Happy Place." Picture in your mind your happy place…where you are calm, your troubles are few, and you have a peaceful smile on your face. You see someone walking toward you, but you don't recognize Him. This man calls out to you, and suddenly you realize…

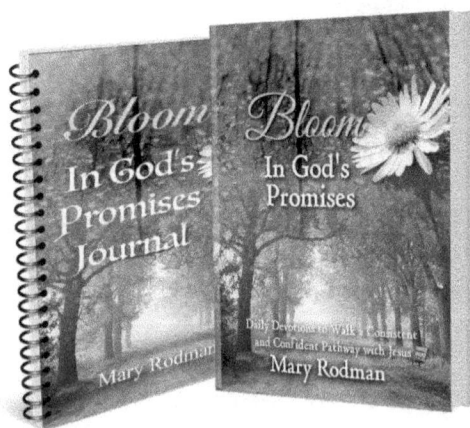

About the Author

Mary resides in Radnor, Ohio with her husband, Jim. Together they enjoy farm life, hard work, vacations, family and friends. She is a farm girl who discovered her niche as a Christian author and speaker. Mary loves sharing about the Lord through both her written and spoken words. Mary's life is an open book as she shares her joys, struggles and embarrassing moments.

As a Christian author and speaker, Mary's objective is to point you toward Jesus. Her words are simple, and her examples are relatable, but when Jesus touches your heart it is amazing. When you follow Him wholeheartedly, and align your dreams with God's will, the outcome is life altering.

The first goal of Mary's ministry is to offer you encouragement and inspiration. She is a "seed planter." The person who sees a glimmer of hope in the small day-to-day routines of life. Therefore, the key verse for her ministry is: *"When we get together, I want to encourage you in your faith, but I also want to be encouraged by yours." (Romans 1:12).*

Once the seed of hope is planted in your heart, Mary motivates you to stay in God's Word to seek wisdom, and learn more about Jesus' amazing grace. *"If you need wisdom, ask our generous God, and he will give it to you. He will not rebuke you for asking." (James 1:5).*

Mary's prayer is that you have a personal relationship with our Redeemer, because when you *Bloom* with Jesus, you become a child of God who is cultivated for your beauty. This beauty does not happen overnight, it is a gradual change within your soul, because of your relationship with Jesus.

For more information of God's grace, go to https://maryrodman.com/gods-promises/[1].

---

[1] https://maryrodman.com/gods-promises/

About The Publisher

We love helping heart-centered, Christian-principled aspiring writers, and new authors tell your compelling stories and showcase your excellence like no other. Our publishing ministry is designed to help you whether you've already written your book, or it's still a vision or a dream.

Our Promise

You retain full control over your manuscripts, cover design, and editing options. You may publish your completed project in any or all formats available. You retain full copyright privileges to all manuscripts, cover designs, or other print materials produced while working with us. You retain the freedom to publish in all languages, globally.

Legacy Lane Publishing
www.LegacyLanePublisng.com[2]

---

[2] https://LegacyLanePublishing.com

Endnotes

New Living Translation
Unless otherwise indicated, all Scripture quotations are taken from the Holy Bible, New Living Translation, copyright © 1996, 2004, 2007 by Tyndale House Foundation. Used by permission of Tyndale House Publishers, Inc., Carol Stream, Illinois 60188. All rights reserved.